TROPICAL DESIGN

daab

Architects / Designers	Location	City	Page
INTRODUCTION			4
Ramiro Alatorre	Ikal del Mar	Riviera Maya	10
Architrave Design & Planning	Banyan Tree Seychelles	Mahé, Intendance Bay	16
Becker Arquitectos	Residencial Eugenio Sue 208	Mexico City	22
BEDMaR & Shi	Bistro Bar	Singapore	26
Bensley Design Studios Bunnag Architects	Four Seasons Resort Langkawi	Langkawi	32
Mario Biselli, Artur Katchborian - arquitetos	LPVM House	São Sebastião	38
Duangrit Bunnag	Costa Lanta	Krabi	44
flavia cancian + renata furlanetto	House in Araçoiaba	Araçoiaba da Serra	48
Central de Arquitectura	Hotel Deseo	Playa del Carmen	54
Gomez Crespo Arquitectos	Coyoacan House	Mexico City	60
	GM House	Mexico City	64
	Rodavento Hotel	Valle de Bravo	68
	Sierra del Mar House	Puerto Vallarta	74
datumzero design office	ACHIO HOUSE	Santa Ana, San Jose	80
	G HOUSE	Fort Lee, New Jersey	84
Denniston	The Chedi Muscat	Muscat	90
Nayantara Fonseka	Taru Villas' Taprobana	Bentota	96
José Forjaz Arquitectos	Paulino Residence	Maputo	102
Atelier Cosmas Gozali	Origami House	Bandung	108
Grain & Green	Audrey House	Semarang	114
	Honeymoon Suite	Bali	118
	Suite Villa at The Kerobokan	Bali	122
Kerry Hill Architects	Amanwella	Tangalle	128
InFORM Architects	Steer Engineering Corp. Office	Bangalore	134
	Tillany Fine Arts Museum	Bagalur	140
Márcio Kogan	BR House	Araras	144
	Quinta's House	Bragança Paulista	150
Legorreta+Legorreta	La Cruz House	El Tamarindo, Jalisco	156
	Las Terrazas House	El Tamarindo, Jalisco	162
	The Sisters House	Valle de Bravo	168
	Zocalo Residential Compound	Santa Fe	172
Mistry Architects	Sen's Residence	Bangalore	176
MMBB Arquitectos	Clínica de Odontologia	Orlândia	182
Jorge E. Neira + Holly E. Worton	Azulik	Tulum	192
Nitsche Associados	Barra do Sahy Beach House	São Sebastião	198
Stephane Paumier architect DPLG, SPA DESIGN PVT LTD	Extension of the French Institute	Pondicherry	204

Architects / Designers	Location	City	Page
Per Aquum			
Resorts • Spas • Residences	Huvafen Fushi	North Malé Atoll	208
Nick Plewman	Lake Manyara Tree Lodge	Lake Manyara National Park	216
Silvio Rech . Lesley Carstens			
Architecture & Interior Architecture	Mombo Camp	Mombo Island	222
	North Island	North Island	226
Patrick Rendradjaja Architect	Albert's House	Jakarta	232
	K Residence	Jakarta	238
Ricardo Rojas Arquitectos	Casa en la Cima	Acapulco	244
	Villa Cambaros	Acapulco	250
Rojkind Arquitectos			
with Derek Dellekamp	Falcon Headquarters	Mexico City	254
Anthony Russell	Shompole Lodge	Magadi Area Rift Valley	258
Rajiv Saini + Associates	Agarwal House	Bombay	262
	Samudra Mahal	Bombay	268
	Singhania House	Delhi	274
Carmelina Santoro	Laluna	Grenada	282
SCDA Architects Pte Ltd	Andrew Road House	Singapore	288
	Cassia Drive House	Singapore	294
	Sentosa Cove House	Singapore	300
Mohamed Shafeeg Architecture			
Abacus Interior	Anantara Resort Maldives	Dhigufinolhu	306
Mohamed Shafeeg	Baros Maldives	Nord Malé Atoll	312
Simple Space Design Co. Ltd.	Aleenta Resort and Spa and Aleenta Villas	Pilai Beach, Kok Kloy	318
Geewaka De Soyza Associates	Saman Villas	Bentota	324
Bruno Stagno Arquitecto	Holcim Costa Rica	San Rafael	330
	Pergola Building (Agencia Tribu)	San Antonio de Belén	336
studioarsitektur	Taman Tangkuban Prahu House	Jakarta	342
Studio MORSA	Gingerland Residences	Gingerland	348
Sanders Wang MacLeod Internat. Consortium for Arch. and Urbanism (SWiM-CAU)	Handmade House	Jakarta	354
Taller de Arquitectura X, Alberto Kalach	Biblioteca Vasconcelos	Mexico City	360
Isay Weinfeld Arquitetura	Casa Marrom	São Paulo	366
De Yturbe Arquitectos SC	Costa Baja Resort	La Paz	372
	Izar Golf Country Club	Valle de Bravo	376
Index			382
Imprint			384

INTRODUCTION

'Tropical Design' is not an established architectural style, but a collective description of architecture and interior design in tropical countries, designed by architects from around the equator. The term often calls to mind the association of an island paradise which is an interpretation by the Western world and the tourism industry: A bamboo hut under palm trees, white sandy beaches, crystal clear water and rattan furniture situated on a spacious terrace. However, the tropical architecture presented in this book is more than that.

Rooted in the traditional style of architecture that is typical in these countries and influenced by the European modern style, a unique architectural language has developed that reflects contemporary tendencies and corresponds to the climatic requirements. Designs can be realized here due to the predominant climatic conditions in these latitudes that are the dreams of many builders and architects in the Western realm: bright living areas, roof top terraces, single story structures built on stilts and flowing transitions that are created between the indoor and outdoor areas using open floor plans. Projects such as the "Andrew Road House" by SCDA Architects from India pursue the traditions of European modernists such as Le Corbusier or Henry Klumb and perfect the basic principles of international style in the never-ending summer in the tropics.

As multifaceted as nature in the tropical regions, the architecture in the projects presented here is just as diversified. From "Las Terrazas" by Legorreta+Legoretta glowing under the Mexican sun to the romantic "Anantara" on the Maledives Islands to the spacious and modern "LPVM House" by Biselli e Katchborian in Brasil – The book 'Tropical Design' hopes to offer a small insight into the contemporary style with these and further projects and thus awaken the interest in architecture and design from tropical countries.

,Tropical Design' ist kein feststehender Architekturstil, sondern eine zusammenfassende Bezeichnung für Architektur und Interiordesign in tropischen Ländern, entworfen von Architekten rund um den Äquator. Der Begriff ruft oft die von der westlichen Welt und der Tourismusbranche geprägte Assoziation vom Inselparadies hervor: Eine Bambushütte unter Palmen, weißer Sandstrand, kristallklares Wasser und Rattanmöbel auf der großzügig angelegten Terrasse. Doch die in diesem Buch präsentierte Tropenarchitektur ist mehr als das.

Verwurzelt in der landestypischen, traditionellen Bauweise und beeinflußt durch die europäische Moderne hat sich eine eigene Architektursprache entwickelt, die zeitgenössische Tendenzen widerspiegelt und den besonderen klimatischen Bedingungen entspricht. Durch die vorherrschenden Klimaverhältnisse in diesen Breitengraden sind Entwürfe umsetzbar, die im westlichen Raum oft der Traum vieler Bauherren und Architekten sind: Lichtdurchflutete Wohnräume, Dachterrassen, aufgeständerte eingeschossige Bauten und durch offene Grundrisse erzeugte fließende Übergänge zwischen Innen- und Außenraum. Projekte wie das „Andrew Road House" von SCDA Architekten aus Indien stehen in der Tradition europäischer Modernisten wie Le Corbusier oder Henry Klumb und führen die Grundprinzipien des internationalen Stils im immerwährenden Sommer der Tropen zur Perfektion.

So vielfältig die Natur der tropischen Regionen ist, so abwechslungsreich zeigt sich die Architektur der hier vorgestellten Projekte. Von den in der Sonne Mexikos leuchtenden „Las Terrazas" von Legorreta+Legoretta über das romantische „Anantara" auf den Malediven bis hin zur großzügigen und modernen „LPVM House" von Biselli e Katchborian in Brasilien- Das Buch ,Tropical Design' möchte anhand dieser und weiterer Projekte einen kleinen Einblick in den dortigen zeitgenössischen Stil bieten und so das Interesse an Architektur und Design aus den tropischen Ländern wecken.

'Tropical Design' no es un estilo definido de arquitectura, sino una denominación integradora de la arquitectura y el diseño de interiores de países tropicales, creaciones de arquitectos de esos países.

Es una denominación que evoca una asociación común en el resto del mundo y la industria del turismo: una isla paradisíaca, una choza de cañas rodeada de palmeras, arenas blancas, aguas cristalinas y muebles de mimbre en una amplia terraza. Pero la arquitectura tropical presentada en este libro es más que eso.

Con raíces en el modo de construcción típico de cada país e influencias de la modernidad europea, se ha desarrollado un lenguaje arquitectónico propio que refleja tendencias contemporáneas y responde a las condiciones climáticas particulares de la zona. Las características del clima dominantes en estas latitudes permiten crear diseños con los que suelen soñar los propietarios y arquitectos del resto del mundo: salas inundadas de luz natural, azoteas, edificios elevados de un solo nivel, y pasos entre los ambientes interiores y exteriores formados por planos abiertos. Proyectos como la "Andrew Road House" del estudio SCDA de la India siguen la tradición de modernistas europeos como Le Corbusier o Henry Klumb, llevando los principios básicos del estilo internacional en el eterno verano tropical a su concreción más perfecta.

Así como la naturaleza de las regiones tropicales es muy variada, la arquitectura de los proyectos aquí presentados es muy diversa. Desde "Las Terrazas" de Legorreta+Legorreta, iluminadas por el sol de México, pasando por el romántico "Anantara" en las Maledivas, hasta la amplia y moderna "LPVM House" de Biselli e Katchborian, en Brasil, el libro 'Tropical Design', mediante estos y otros proyectos, echa una breve mirada al estilo contemporáneo local y logra así despertar el interés sobre la arquitectura y el diseño de los países tropicales.

'Tropical Design' n'est pas un style architectural défini, mais un terme générique désignant l'architecture et la décoration intérieure dans les pays tropicaux telles que des architectes domiciliés des deux côtés de la ligne équatoriale ont pu les imaginer.

L'expression 'Tropical Design' conduit souvent les Occidentaux et le secteur touristique à lui associer spontanément la notion de paradis insulaire. Une case de bambous sous les palmiers, une plage de sable blanc, de l'eau limpide comme le cristal, des meubles en rotin sur la terrasse généreusement aménagée. L'architecture tropicale pourtant, présentée dans ce livre, c'est plus que cela.

Enraciné dans la construction traditionnelle typique du pays et influencé par la modernité européenne, tout un langage architectural s'est développé qui reflète les tendances contemporaines et s'adapte aux conditions climatiques particulières. Celles prévalant sous ces latitudes permettent de concrétiser les études objets des rêves, dans le monde occidental, de nombreux maîtres d'ouvrage et architectes: des séjours baignés de lumière, des toitures-terrasses, des constructions d'un étage sur pilotis et des transitions fluides, permises par des plans d'ensemble ouverts, entre l'espace intérieur et l'espace extérieur. Des projets comme l'« Andrew Road House » de SCDA Architects en Inde se situent dans la lignée des modernistes européens comme Le Corbusier ou Henry Klumb et portent à la perfection les principes fondamentaux du style international sous l'éternel soleil des tropiques.

L'architecture propre aux projets présentés ici est tout aussi diversifiée que la Nature des régions tropicales qui l'hébergent. Des « Las Terrazas » de Legoretta+Legoretta sous le soleil mexicain à la moderne et vaste «LPVM House» de Biselli e Katchborian au Brésil, en passant par la romantique « Anantara » aux Maldives, cet ouvrage, 'Tropical Design', souhaite à l'aide de ces projets ainsi que d'autres, livrer un petit aperçu du style contemporain qui y est pratiqué et éveiller au passage l'intérêt pour l'architecture et le design en provenance de ces pays.

Il 'Tropical Design' non è uno stile architettonico definito, bensì un termine riepilogativo che sta per l'architettura e l'interior design dei paesi tropicali, creati da architetti attorno all'Equatore.

Questo termine spesso fa suscitare l'immagine di isole paradisiache, coniato dal mondo occidentale e dal settore turistico: una capanna di bambù sotto le palme, una spiaggia di sabbia bianca, acqua limpida e mobili in rattan su un ampio terrazzo. L'architettura tropicale presentata in questo volume va invece oltre.

Radicato nelle costruzioni locali tradizionali ed influenzato dall'architettura moderna europea, si è sviluppato un proprio linguaggio architettonico che riflette le tendenze contemporanee nel rispetto delle particolari condizioni climatiche. Grazie al clima presente in questi gradi di latitudine, diventano realizzabili quei concetti di cui molti committenti ed architetti dei paesi dell'Ovest spesso sognano: vani immersi nella luce, terrazze sul tetto, costruzioni ad un solo piano rialzate su pali e piante costruttive aperte che permettono passaggi fluidi dall'interno verso l'esterno. Progetti come l' "Andrew Road House" degli architetti dell'indiana SCDA rispecchiano la tradizione dei Modernisti europei come Le Corbusier oppure Henry Klumb e portano i principi base dello stile internazionale alla perfezione nell'estate eterna dei tropicali.

Quanto è ricca la natura delle regioni tropicali, tanto è varia l'architettura dei progetti presentati qui. Dalle terrazze "Las Terrazas" di Legorreta+Legoretta illuminate dal sole messicano, attraverso il romantico "Anantara" sulle isole delle Maldive fino alla generosa e moderna "LPVM House" di Biselli e Katchborian in Brasile – il volume 'Tropical Design' con questi ed altri progetti offre uno sguardo sullo stile locale contemporaneo ed intende svegliare così l'interesse per l'architettura e il design nei paesi tropicali.

RAMIRO ALATORRE | **MEXICO CITY**
Ikal del Mar
Riviera Maya, Mexico | 2002

ARCHITRAVE DESIGN & PLANNING | SINGAPORE
Banyan Tree Seychelles
Mahé, Intendance Bay, Seychelles

BECKER ARQUITECTOS | MEXICO CITY
Residencial Eugenio Sue 208
Mexico City, Mexico | 2003

BEDMAR & SHI | SINGAPORE
Bistro Bar
Singapore | 2006

BENSLEY DESIGN STUDIOS | BANGKOK
BUNNAG ARCHITECTS | BANGKOK
Four Seasons Resort Langkawi
Langkawi, Kedah Darul Aman, Malaysia | 2005

MARIO BISELLI, ARTUR KATCHBORIAN - ARQUITETOS | SÃO PAULO
LPVM House
São Sebastião, Brazil | 2005

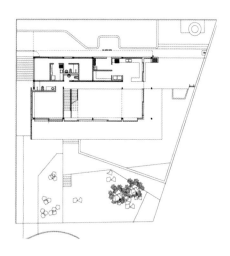

DUANGRIT BUNNAG | BANGKOK
Costa Lanta
Krabi, Thailand | 2002

FLAVIA CANCIAN +
RENATA FURLANETTO | ARAÇOIABA DA SERRA
House in Araçoiaba
Araçoiaba da Serra, Brazil | 2004

CENTRAL DE ARQUITECTURA | MEXICO CITY
Hotel Deseo
Playa del Carmen, Quintana Roo, Mexico | 2002

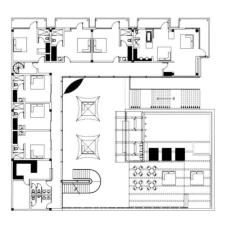

GOMEZ CRESPO ARQUITECTOS | MEXICO CITY
Coyoacan House
Mexico City, Mexico | 2004

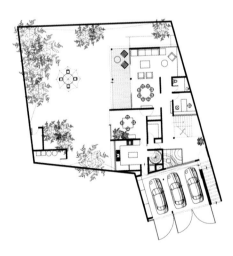

GOMEZ CRESPO ARQUITECTOS | MEXICO CITY
GM House
Mexico City, Mexico | 2001

GOMEZ CRESPO ARQUITECTOS | **MEXICO CITY**
Rodavento Hotel
Valle de Bravo, Edo. de Mexico, Mexico | 2004

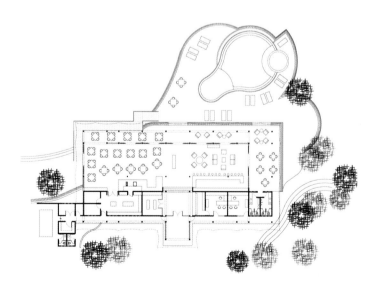

GOMEZ CRESPO ARQUITECTOS | **MEXICO CITY**
Sierra del Mar House
Puerto Vallarta, Jalisco, Mexico | 2000

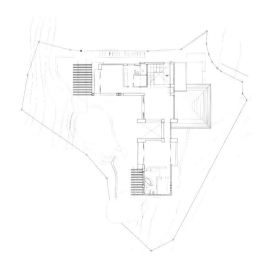

DATUMZERO DESIGN OFFICE | **SAN JOSÉ, COSTA RICA**
ACHIO HOUSE
Santa Ana, San José, Costa Rica | 1999

DATUMZERO DESIGN OFFICE I **SAN JOSÉ, COSTA RICA**
G HOUSE
Fort Lee, New Jersey I 2005

DENNISTON | SINGAPORE
The Chedi Muscat
Muscat, Sultanate of Oman | 2002

NAYANTARA FONSEKA | COLOMBO
Taru Villas' Taprobana
Bentota, Sri Lanka | 2002

JOSÉ FORJAZ ARQUITECTOS | **MAPUTO**
Paulino Residence
Maputo, Mozambique | 2004

ATELIER COSMAS GOZALI | **JAKARTA**
Origami House
Bandung, Indonesia | 1999

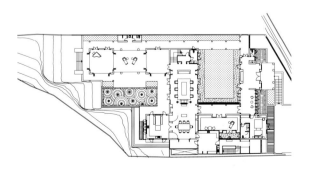

GRAIN & GREEN | JAKARTA
Honeymoon Suite at Kayu Manis Private Villa
Bali, Indonesia | 2004

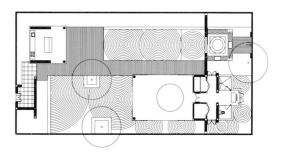

GRAIN & GREEN | JAKARTA
Suite Villa at The Kerobokan
Bali, Indonesia | 2006

KERRY HILL ARCHITECTS | **SINGAPORE**
Amanwella
Tangalle, Sri Lanka | 2005

INFORM ARCHITECTS | BANGALORE
Steer Engineering Corporate Office
Bangalore, India | 2003

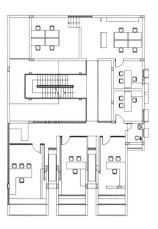

INFORM ARCHITECTS | **BANGALORE**
Tillany Fine Arts Museum & Gallery
The George Foundation
Bagalur, Tamil Nadu India | 2001

MÁRCIO KOGAN | **SÃO PAULO**
Quinta's House
Bragança Paulista, Brazil | 2004

LEGORRETA+LEGORRETA | MEXICO CITY
La Cruz House
El Tamarindo, Jalisco, Mexico | 2000

LEGORRETA+LEGORRETA | **MEXICO CITY**
Las Terrazas House
El Tamarindo, Jalisco, Mexico | 2001

LEGORRETA+LEGORETTA | MEXICO CITY
The Sisters House
Valle de Bravo, Mexico | 2002

LEGORRETA+LEGORRETA | **MEXICO CITY**
Zocalo Residential Compound
Santa Fe, New Mexico | 2005

MISTRY ARCHITECTS | **BANGALORE**
Sen's Residence
Bangalore, India | 2003

MMBB ARQUITECTOS | SÃO PAULO
Clínica de Odontologia
Orlândia, Brazil | 2000

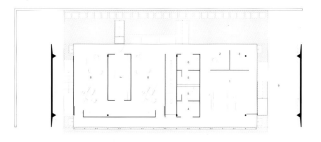

JORGE E. NEIRA + HOLLY E. WORTON
Azulik
Tulum, Mexico I 2003

NITSCHE ASSOCIADOS | SÃO SEBASTIÃO
Barra do Sahy Beach House
São Sebastião, Brazil | 2003

**STEPHANE PAUMIER ARCHITECT DPLG,
SPA DESIGN PVT LTD | NEW DELHI**
Extension of the French Institute of Pondicherry
Pondicherry, India | 2003

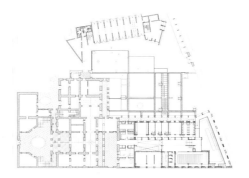

PER AQUUM RESORTS • SPAS • RESIDENCES | HUVAFEN FUSHI
Huvafen Fushi
North Malé Atoll, Maldives | 2004

NICK PLEWMAN | JOHANNESBURG
Lake Manyara Tree Lodge
Lake Manyara National Park, Tanzania | 2001

**SILVIO RECH . LESLEY CARSTENS ARCHITECTURE
& INTERIOR ARCHITECTURE | JOHANNESBURG**
Mombo Camp
Mombo Island, Botswana | 2000

SILVIO RECH . LESLEY CARSTENS ARCHITECTURE & INTERIOR ARCHITECTURE | JOHANNESBURG
North Island
North Island, Seychelles | 2003

PATRICK RENDRADJAJA ARCHITECT | JAKARTA
Albert's House
Jakarta, Indonesia | 2005

PATRICK RENDRADJAJA ARCHITECT | **JAKARTA**
K Residence
Jakarta, Indonesia | 2003

RICARDO ROJAS ARQUITECTOS | ACAPULCO
Casa en la Cima
Acapulco, Mexico | 2004

RICARDO ROJAS ARQUITECTOS | ACAPULCO
Villa Cambaros
Acapulco, Mexico | 2002

ROJKIND ARQUITECTOS
WITH DEREK DELLEKAMP | MEXICO CITY
Falcon Headquarters
Mexico City, Mexico | 2004

ANTHONY RUSSELL | NAIROBI
Shompole Lodge
Magadi Area Rift Valley, Kenya | 2001

RAJIV SAINI + ASSOCIATES | BOMBAY
Agarwal House
Bombay, India | 2005

RAJIV SAINI + ASSOCIATES | BOMBAY
Samudra Mahal
Bombay, India | 2003

RAJIV SAINI + ASSOCIATES | **BOMBAY**
Singhania House
Delhi, India | 2003

CARMELINA SANTORO | NEW YORK CITY
Laluna
Grenada, West Indies | 2000

SCDA ARCHITECTS PTE LTD | SINGAPORE
Andrew Road House
Singapore | 2003

SCDA ARCHITECTS PTE LTD | SINGAPORE
Cassia Drive House
Singapore | 2004

SCDA ARCHITECTS PTE LTD | SINGAPORE
Sentosa Cove House
Singapore | 2006

MOHAMED SHAFEEG ARCHITECTURE | MALDIVES
ABACUS INTERIOR | THAILAND
Anantara Resort Maldives
Dhigufinolhu, South Malé Atoll, Maldives | 2006

MOHAMED SHAFEEG | **MALDIVES**
Baros Maldives
North Malé Atoll, Maldives | 2005

SIMPLE SPACE DESIGN CO. LTD. | BANGKOK
Aleenta Resort and Spa and Aleenta Villas
Pilai Beach, Kok Kloy, Phangnga | 2006

GEEWAKA DE SOYZA ASSOCIATES | COLOMBO
Saman Villas
Bentota, Sri Lanka | 1995

BRUNO STAGNO ARQUITECTO | **SAN JOSÉ, COSTA RICA**
Holcim Costa Rica
San Rafael, Alajuela, Costa Rica | 2004

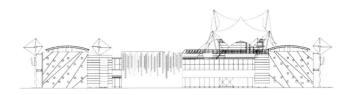

BRUNO STAGNO ARQUITECTO | **SAN JOSÉ, COSTA RICA**
Pergola Building (Agencia Tribu)
San Antonio de Belén, Heredia, Costa Rica | 2004

STUDIOARSITEKTUR | JAKARTA
Taman Tangkuban Prahu House
Jakarta, Indonesia | 2006

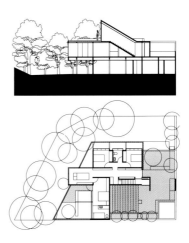

STUDIO MORSA | NEW YORK CITY
Gingerland Residences
Gingerland, Nevis, West Indies | 1992

**SANDERS WANG MACLEOD INTERNATIONAL CONSORTIUM
FOR ARCHITECTURE AND URBANISM (SWIM-CAU) I JAKARTA**
Handmade House
Jakarta, Indonesia I 2004

TALLER DE ARQUITECTURA X, ALBERTO KALACH | MEXICO CITY
Biblioteca Vasconcelos
Mexico City, Mexico | 2006

ISAY WEINFELD ARQUITETURA | SÃO PAULO
Casa Marrom
São Paulo, Brazil | 2004

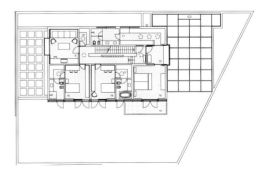

DE YTURBE ARQUITECTOS SC | MEXICO CITY
Costa Baja Resort
La Paz, Mexico | 2005

DE YTURBE ARQUITECTOS SC | MEXICO CITY
Izar Golf Country Club
Valle de Bravo, Mexico | 1999

INDEX

Ramiro Alatorre | Mexico City
Photos: Martin Nicholas Kunz   10

Architrave Design & Planning | Singapore
Photos: Martin Nicholas Kunz   16

Becker Arquitectos | Mexico City
www.beckerarquitectos.com
Photos: Fernando Cordero   22

BEDMaR & Shi | Singapore
www.bedmar-and-shi.com
Photos: Albert Lim KS   26

Bensley Design Studios | Bangkok
Bunnag Architects | Bangkok
www.bensley.com
Photos: Markus Gortz and Four Seasons Resort   32

Mario Biselli, Artur Katchborian
- arquitetos | São Paulo
Photos: Nelson Kon   38

Duangrit Bunnag | Bangkok
Photos: Courtesy of Costa Lanta   44

flavia cancian +
renata furlanetto | Araçoiaba da Serra
Photos: Nelson Kon   48

Central de Arquitectura | Mexico City
www.centraldearquitectura.com
Photos: Luís Gordoa   54

Gomez Crespo Arquitectos | Mexico City
www.gomezcrespoarquitectos.com
Photos: Alfonso de Bèjar   60, 68
Photos: Editorial Basilisco   64
Photos: Eduardo Solórzano, Hector Velazco   74

datumzero design office | San José, Costa Rica
www.datumzero.com
Photos: Frank Schwere   80
Photos: Magda Biernat   84

Denniston | Singapore
Photos: Courtesy of The Chedi Muscat   90

Nayantara Fonseka | Colombo
Photos: Gavin Jackson   96

José Forjaz Arquitectos | Maputo
www.joseforjazarquitectos.com
Photos: Filipe Branquinho   102

Atelier Cosmas Gozali | Jakarta
www.ateliercosmas.com
Photos: Courtesy of
Atelier Cosmas Gozali (PT Arya Cipta Graha)   108

Grain & Green | Jakarta
www.grainandgreen.com
Photos: Courtesy of Grain & Green   114, 118, 122

Kerry Hill Architects | Singapore
Photos: Gavin Jackson   128

InFORM Architects | Bangalore
www.informarchitects.com
Photos: S. Vishwanath   134
Photos: Clare Arni   140

Márcio Kogan | São Paulo
www.marciokogan.com.br
Photos: Nelson Kon   144, 150

Legorreta+Legorreta | Mexico City
www.legorretalegorreta.com
Photos: Lourdes Legorreta   156, 162, 168, 172

Mistry Architects | Bangalore
www.mistrys.com
Photos: Sharukh Mistry   176

MMBB arquitectos | São Paulo
www.mmbb.com.br
Photos: Nelson Kon   182

Jorge Eduardo Neira
Holly Elizabeth Worton
Photos: Martin Nicholas Kunz, Michelle Galindo   192

Nitsche Associados | São Sebastião   198
Photos: Nelson Kon

Stephane Paumier architect DPLG,
SPA DESIGN PVT LTD | New Delhi
Photos: F. Delangle   204

Per Aquum
Resorts • Spas • Residences | Huvafen Fushi
Photos: Courtesy of Huvafen Fushi   208

Nick Plewman | Johannesburg
Photos: Heiner Orth   216

Silvio Rech . Lesley Carstens Architecture &
Interior Architecture | Johannesburg
Photos: Martin Nicholas Kunz, Michael Poliza   222
Photos: Courtesy of www.wilderness-safaris.com
Veranstalter Abendsonne Afrika +49 7343-2998-0   226

Patrick Rendradjaja | Jakarta
Photos: Albert Widjaja   232
Photos: Indra D. Phangandy   238

Ricardo Rojas Arquitectos | Acapulco
www.ricardorojasarquitectos.com
Photos: Luís Gordoa   244
Photos: Claudia Rojas García Travesi   248

Rojkind Arquitectos
with Derek Dellekamp | Mexico City
www.rojkindarquitectos.com
www.dellekamparq.com
Photos: Jaime Navarro   254

Anthony Russell | Nairobi
Photos: Courtesy of Shompole Lodge – Kenya   258

Rajiv Saini + Associates | Bombay
www.rajivsaini.com
Photos: Courtesy of Rajiv Saini + Associates   262, 268, 274

Carmelina Santoro | **New York City**
Photos: Martin Nicholas Kunz   282

SCDA Architects Pte Ltd | **Singapore**
www.scdaarchitects.com
Photos: Albert Lim KS   288, 300
Photos: Harshan Thomson   294

Mohamed Shafeeg Architecture | **Maldives**
Abacus Interior | **Thailand**
Photos: Gavin Jackson   306

Mohamed Shafeeg | **Maldives**
Photos: Gavin Jackson   312

Simple Space Design Co. Ltd. | **Bangkok**
Photos: Courtesy of Aleenta   318

Geewaka De Soyza Associates | **Colombo**
Photos: Gavin Jackson   324

Bruno Stagno Arquitecto | **San José, Costa Rica**
www.brunostagno.info
Photos: Bruno Stagno, Jimena Ugarte   330
Photos: Bruno Stagno, Ronald Valverde   336

studioarsitektur | **Jakarta**
Photos: Adi Purnomo   342

Studio MORSA | **New York City**
Photos: Antoine Bootz   348

Sanders Wang MacLeod International Consortium
for Architecture and Urbanism (SWiM-CAU) | **Jakarta**
www.swimcau.com
Photos: Courtesy of Albertus Wang (SWiM-CAU)   354

Taller de Arquitectura X,
Alberto Kalach | **Mexico City**
www.kalach.com
Photos: Michelle Galindo, Martin Nicholas Kunz   360

Isay Weinfeld Arquitetura | **São Paulo**
www.isayweinfeld.com
Photos: Christiano Mascaro   366

De Yturbe Arquitectos SC | **Mexico City**
www.deyturbe.com
Photos: Fernando Cordero   372
Photos: Michael Calderwood   376

© 2007 daab
cologne   london   new york

published and distributed worldwide by
daab gmbh
friesenstr. 50
d - 50670 köln

p + 49 - 221 - 913 927 0
f   + 49 - 221 - 913 927 20

mail@daab-online.com
www.daab-online.com

publisher ralf daab
rdaab@daab-online.com

creative director feyyaz
mail@feyyaz.com

editorial project by fusion publishing gmbh stuttgart . los angeles
© 2007 fusion publishing, www.fusion-publishing.com

editor anne dörte schmidt

layout anne dörte schmidt
imaging jan hausberg, martin herterich

photo credits
coverphoto courtesy of huvafen fushi
introduction page 7 albert lim ks, 8 courtesy of grain & green, 9 nelson kon
text introduction anne dörte schmidt
translations by ade team übersetzungen / stuttgart, claudia ade
english translation claudia ade
french translation dominique santoro
spanish translation sara costa-sengera
italian translation jacqueline rizzo

printed in italy
www.zanardi.it

isbn 978 - 3 - 937718 - 68 - 2